YOU CAN BE
Everything
GOD WANTS YOU TO BE

MAX LUCADO

THOMAS NELSON
Since 1798

NASHVILLE   DALLAS   MEXICO CITY   RIO DE JANEIRO   BEIJING

"... I know what I'm doing.

I have it all planned out—

plans to take care of you,

not abandon you,

PLANS TO GIVE YOU THE FUTURE

YOU HOPE FOR.*"

JEREMIAH 29:10–11 MSG

MAX LUCADO, Minister of Preaching for the Oak Hills Church in San Antonio, Texas, is the husband of Denalyn and father of Jenna, Andrea, and Sara. In a good week he reads a good book, has a few dinners with his wife, and breaks 90 on the golf course. He usually settles for the first two.

Selections in this book are taken from
Cure for the Common Life.

FIND YOUR
Sweet Spot

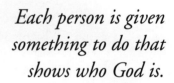

*Each person is given
something to do that
shows who God is.*

1 CORINTHIANS 12:7 MSG

"SWEET SPOT." Golfers understand the term. So do tennis players. Ever swung a baseball bat or paddled a Ping-Pong ball? If so, you know the oh-so-nice feel of the sweet spot. Connect with these prime inches of real estate and *kapow!* The collective technologies of the universe afterburn the ball into orbit, leaving you Frisbee eyed and strutting. Your arm doesn't tingle, and the ball doesn't ricochet. Your boyfriend remembers birthdays, the tax refund comes early, and the flight attendant bumps you up to first class. Life in the sweet spot rolls like the downhill side of a downwind bike ride.

But you don't have to swing a bat or a club to know this. What engineers give sports equipment, God gave you. A zone, a region, a life precinct in which you were made to dwell. He tailored the curves of your life to fit an empty space in his jigsaw puzzle. And life makes sweet sense when you find your spot. But how do you? Where do you go? What pills do you order, class do you take, or infomercial do you watch? None of the above. Simply quarry . . .

YOUR UNIQUENESS.

Da Vinci painted one Mona Lisa.

Beethoven composed one Fifth Symphony.

And God made one version of you. He custom designed you for a one-of-a-kind assignment. Mine like a gold digger the unique-to-you nuggets from your life.

When I was six years old, my father built us a house. *Architectural Digest* didn't notice, but my mom sure did. Dad constructed it, board by board, every day after work. My youth didn't deter him from giving me a job. He tied an empty nail apron around my waist, placed a magnet in my hands, and sent me on daily patrols around the building site, carrying my magnet only inches off the ground.

One look at my tools and you could guess my job. Stray-nail collector.

One look at yours and the same can be said. Brick by brick, life by life, God is creating a kingdom, a "spiritual house" (1 Pet. 2:5 CEV). He entrusted you with a key task in the project. Examine your tools and discover it. Your ability unveils your destiny. "If anyone ministers, let him do it as *with the ability which God supplies*, that in all things God may be glorified through Jesus Christ" (1 Pet. 4:11). When God gives an assignment, he also gives the skill. Study your skills, then, to reveal your assignment.

Look at you. Your uncanny ease with numbers. Your quenchless curiosity about chemistry. Others stare at blueprints and yawn; you read them and drool. "I was made to do this," you say.

Heed that inner music. No one else hears it the way you do.

FIND YOUR
Uniqueness

And to one he gave five talents,
to another two,
and to another one,
to each according
to his own ability.

MATTHEW 25:25

AT THIS VERY MOMENT in another section of the church building in which I write, little kids explore their tools. Preschool classrooms may sound like a cacophony to you and me, but God hears a symphony.

A five-year-old sits at a crayon-strewn table. He seldom talks. Classmates have long since set aside their papers, but he ponders his. The colors compel him. He marvels at the gallery of kelly green and navy blue and royal purple. Masterpiece in hand, he'll race to Mom and Dad, eager to show them his kindergarten Picasso.

His sister, however, forgets her drawing. She won't consume the home commute with tales of painted pictures. She'll tell tales of tales. "The teacher told us a new story today!" And the girl will need no prodding to repeat it.

Another boy cares less about the story and the drawings and more about the other kids. He spends the day wearing a "Hey, listen to me!" expression, lingering at the front of the class, testing the patience of the teacher. He relishes attention, evokes reactions. His theme seems to be "Do it this way. Come with me. Let's try this."

Meaningless activities at an insignificant age?

Or subtle hints of hidden strengths? I opt for the latter. The quiet boy with the color fascination may someday brighten city walls with murals. His sister may pen a screenplay or teach literature to curious coeds. And the kid who recruits followers today might eventually do the same on behalf of a product, the poor, or even his church.

What about you? Our Maker gives assignments to people, "to each according to each one's unique ability" (Matt. 25:15).[1] As he calls, he equips. Look back over your life.

You have one. A divine spark.

What have you consistently done well? What have you loved to do? Stand at the intersection of your affections and successes and find your uniqueness.

You have one. A divine spark.[2] An uncommon call to an uncommon life. "The Spirit has given each of us a *special way* of serving others" (1 Cor. 12:7 CEV). So much for the excuse "I don't have anything to offer." Did the apostle Paul say, "The Spirit has given *some* of us . . ."? Or, "The Spirit has given a *few* of us . . ."? No. "The Spirit has given *each of us* a special way of serving others." Enough of this self-deprecating "I can't do anything."

And enough of its arrogant opposite: "I have to do everything." No, you don't! You're not God's solution to society, but a solution in society. Imitate Paul, who said, "Our goal is to stay within the boundaries of God's plan for us" (2 Cor. 10:13 NLT). Clarify your contribution.

MAGNIFY
Your Maker

*Each person is given
something to do
that shows who God is.*

1 COR. 12:7 MSG

DON'T WORRY about skills you don't have. Don't covet strengths others do have. Just extract your uniqueness. "Kindle afresh the gift of God which is in you" (2 Tim. 1:6 NASB). And do so to . . .

MAKE A BIG DEAL OUT OF GOD.

"Everything comes from God alone. Everything lives by his power, and everything is for his glory" (Rom. 11:36 TLB). The breath you just took? God gave that. The blood that just pulsed through your heart? Credit God. The light by which you read and the brain with which you process? He gave both.

Everything comes from him . . . and exists for him. We exist to exhibit God, to display his glory. We serve as canvases for his brush stroke, papers for his pen, soil for his seeds, glimpses of his image.

Texas A&M's T-shirted football fans model our role. In the aftermath of September 11, many Americans sought an opportunity to demonstrate patriotism and solidarity. Five students set the pace. They designated the next home football game as Red, White, and Blue Out and sold T-shirts to each of the seventy thousand fans. Kyle Field morphed into a human flag as those seated in the third deck wore red, the second deck wore white, and the lower deck wore blue. Newspapers across America splashed the picture on front pages.[3]

Newsworthy indeed! How often do thousands of people billboard a singular, powerful message? God fashioned us to do so for him. He distributes, not shirts, but strengths. He sends people, not to bleacher seats, but to life assignments: "Go to your place. Dispatch your abilities, and unfurl my goodness."

God endows us with gifts so we can make him known.

Most refuse. Few cooperate. We accept the present, but neglect its purpose. We accept the gift, thank you, but ignore the Giver and promote self. Why, some of us have been known to parade up and down the aisles, shouting, "Hey, look at me!"

Need an explanation for the anarchy in the world? You just read it. When you center-stage your gifts and I pump my image and no one gives a lick about honoring God, dare we expect anything short of chaos?

God endows us with gifts so we can make him known. Period. God endues the Olympian with speed, the salesman with savvy, the surgeon with skill. Why? For gold medals, closed sales, or healed bodies? Only partially.

The big answer is to make a big to-do out of God. Brandish him. Herald him. "God has given gifts to each of you from his great variety of spiritual gifts. Manage them well. . . . *Then God will be given glory*" (1 Pet. 4:10–11 NLT).

Live so that "he'll get all the credit as the One mighty in everything—encores to the end of time. Oh, yes!" (1 Pet. 4:11 MSG). Exhibit God with your uniqueness. When you magnify your Maker with your strengths, when your contribution enriches God's reputation, your days grow suddenly sweet. And to really dulcify your world, use your uniqueness to make a big deal about God . . .

EVERY DAY OF YOUR LIFE.

YOU HAVE ONE.
*A divine
spark.*

YOUR WORK
Matters

And whatever you do
IN WORD OR DEED,
do all in the name of the Lord Jesus,
giving thanks to God the Father
through Him.

COLOSSIANS 3:17

HEAVEN'S CALENDAR has seven Sundays a week. God sanctifies each day. He conducts holy business at all hours and in all places. He uncommons the common by turning kitchen sinks into shrines, cafés into convents, and nine-to-five workdays into spiritual adventures.

Workdays? Yes, workdays. He ordained your work as something good. Before he gave Adam a wife or a child, even before he gave Adam britches, God gave Adam a job. "Then the LORD God took the man and put him into the garden of Eden to cultivate it and keep it" (Gen. 2:15 NASB). Innocence, not indolence, characterized the first family.

God views work worthy of its own engraved commandment: "You shall work six days, but on the seventh day you shall rest" (Exod. 34:21 NASB). We like the second half of that verse. But emphasis on the day of rest might cause us to miss the command to work: "You *shall* work six days." Whether you work at home or in the marketplace, your work matters to God.

And your work matters to society. We need you! Cities need plumbers. Nations need soldiers. Stoplights break. Bones break. We need people to repair the first and set the second. Someone has to raise kids, raise cane, and manage the kids who raise Cain.

Whether you log on or lace up for the day, you imitate God.

Jehovah himself worked for the first six days of creation. Jesus said, "My Father never stops working, and so I keep working, too" (John 5:17 NCV). Your career consumes half of your lifetime. Shouldn't it broadcast God? Don't those forty to sixty hours a week belong to him as well?

Heaven's calendar has seven Sundays a week.

The Bible never promotes workaholism or an addiction to employment as pain medication. But God unilaterally calls all the physically able to till the gardens he gives. God honors work. So honor God in your work.

"There is nothing better for a man than to eat and drink and tell himself that his labor is good" (Eccles. 2:24 NASB). I just heard a groan. "But, Max," someone objects, "my work is simply that—work! It pays my bills, but numbs my soul." (You're only a few pages from some help.) "Job satisfaction? How about job survival? How do I survive a job misfit?" (I have some ideas.)

"I have no clue how to find my skill." (By the end of the book you will.)

For now, here is the big idea:

Use your uniqueness (what you do) to make a big deal out of God (why you do it) every day of your life (where you do it).

At the convergence of all three, you'll find the cure for the common life: your sweet spot.

Sweet spot. You have one, you know. Your life has a plot; your years have a theme. You can do something in a manner that no one else can. And when you find it and do it, another sweet spot is discovered. Let's find yours.

UNPACK
Your Bag

He has filled them with skill.

EXODUS 35:35 PHILLIPS

YOU WERE BORN PREPACKED. God looked at your entire life, determined your assignment, and gave you the tools to do the job.

Before traveling, you do something similar. You consider the demands of the journey and pack accordingly. Cold weather? Bring a jacket. Business meeting? Carry the laptop. Time with grandchildren? Better take some sneakers and pain medication.

God did the same with you. *Joe will research animals . . . install curiosity. Meagan will lead a private school . . . add an extra dose of management. I need Eric to comfort the sick . . . include a healthy share of compassion. Denalyn will marry Max . . . instill a double portion of patience.*

"Each of us is an original" (Gal. 5:26 MSG). God packed you on purpose for a purpose. Is this news to you? If so, you may be living out of the wrong bag.

I once grabbed the wrong bag at the airport. The luggage looked like mine. Same size. Same material. Same color. Thrilled that it had emerged early from the baggage catacombs, I yanked it off the carousel and headed to the hotel. One glance inside, however, and I knew I'd made a mistake.

Wrong size, style, and gender. (Besides, my pants would be too short with stiletto heels.)

What would you do in such a case? You could make do with what you have. Cram your body into the tight clothes, deck out in other-gender jewelry, and head out for your appointments. But would you? Only at risk of job loss and jail time.

No, you'd hunt down your own bag. Issue an all-points bulletin. Call the airport. Call the airlines. The taxi service. The FBI. Hire bloodhounds and private investigators. You'd try every possible way to find the person who can't find her suitcase and is wondering what gooney bird failed to check the nametag.

God packed you on purpose for a purpose.

No one wants to live out of someone else's bag.

Then why do we? Odds are, someone has urged a force fit into clothes not packed for you.

Parents do. The dad puts an arm around his young son. "Your great-granddad was a farmer. Your granddad was a farmer. I'm a farmer. And you, my son, will someday inherit the farm."

A teacher might. She warns the young girl who wants to be a stay-at-home mom, "Don't squander your skills. With your gifts you could make it to the top. The professional world is the way to go."

Church leaders assign luggage from the pulpit. "God seeks world-changing, globe-trotting missionaries. Jesus was a missionary. Do you want to please your Maker? Follow him into the holy vocation. Spend your life on foreign soil."

Sound counsel or poor advice? That depends on what God packed in the person's bag.

A bequeathed farm blesses the individualist and physically active. But what if God fashioned the farmer's son with a passion for literature or medicine?

Work outside the home might be a great choice for some, but what if God gave the girl a singular passion for kids and homemaking?

Those wired to learn languages and blaze trails should listen up to sermons promoting missionary service. But if foreign cultures frustrate you while predictability invigorates you, would you be happy as a missionary?

DON'T JOIN THE
Dullsville Crowd

If people can't see what God is doing,
they stumble all over themselves;
but when they attend to what he reveals,
they are most blessed.

PROVERBS 29:18 MSG

HERE ARE SOME MIND-NUMBING statistics you don't want to contribute to:

- Unhappiness on the job affects one-fourth of the American work force.[4]

- One-fourth of employees view their jobs as the number-one stressor in their lives.[5]

- Seven out of ten people are neither motivated nor competent to perform the basics of their job.[6]

- Forty-three percent of employees feel anger toward their employers often or very often as a result of feeling overworked.[7]

Did you feel the force of those figures?

Who sucked the sparkle out of our days?

You wonder why workbound commuters seem so cranky? "Fully 70 percent of us go to work without much enthusiasm or passion."[8] Most wage earners spend forty of their eighty waking weekday hours trudging through the streets of Dullsville.

Such misery can't help but sour families, populate bars, and pay the salaries of therapists. If 70 percent of us dread Mondays, dream of Fridays, and slug through the rest of the week, won't our relationships suffer? Won't our work suffer? Won't our health suffer? One study states, "Problems at work are more strongly associated with health complaints than any other life stressor—more so than even financial problems or family problems."[9]

Such numbers qualify as an epidemic. An epidemic of commonness. Someone sucked the sparkle out of our days. A stale fog has settled over our society. Week after week of energy-sapping sameness. Walls painted gray with routine. Commuters dragging their dread to the office. Buildings packed with people working to live rather than living to work. Boredom. Mediocre performance.

God
packed you
on purpose
FOR A

PURPOSE

Be You-nique

I was woven together in the dark of the womb.

PSALM 139:15 NLT

THE CURE for getting and staying out of Dullsville? God's prescription begins with unpacking your bags. You exited the womb uniquely equipped. David states it this way: "My frame was not hidden from you when I was made in the secret place. When I was woven together in the depths of the earth, your eyes saw my unformed body. All the days ordained for me were written in your book before one of them came to be" (Ps. 139:15–16 NIV).

Spelunk these verses with me. David emphasizes the pronoun "you" as if to say "you, God, and you alone." "The secret place" suggests a hidden and safe place, concealed from intruders and evil. Just as an artist takes a canvas into a locked studio, so

God took you into his hidden chamber where you were "woven together." Moses used the same word to describe the needlework of the tabernacle's inner curtains—stitched together by skillful hands for the highest purpose (see Exod. 26:1; 36:8; 38:9). The Master Weaver selected your temperament threads, your character texture, the yarn of your personality—all before you were born. God did not drop you into the world utterly defenseless and empty-handed. You arrived fully equipped. "All the days ordained . . ." Day of birth and day of death. Days of difficulty and victory. What motivates you, what exhausts you . . . God authored—and authors—it all.

Other translations employ equally intriguing verbs:

> You . . . knit me together. (v. 13 NLT)
> I was . . . intricately and curiously wrought [as if embroidered with various colors]. (v. 15 AMP)

My hands have never embroidered a stitch, but my mom's have. In pre-dishwasher days when mothers drafted young sons into kitchen duty to dry dishes, I grew too acquainted with her set of embroidered dishtowels. She had embellished sturdy white cloths with colorful threads: seven towels, each bearing the name of a different day. Her artisan skills rendered common towels uncommonly unique.

God did the same with you! Don't dull your life by missing this point: You are more than statistical chance, more than a marriage of heredity and society, more than a confluence of inherited chromosomes and childhood trauma. More than a walking weather vane whipped about by the cold winds of fate. Thanks to God, you have been "sculpted from nothing into something" (v. 15 MSG).

Envision Rodin carving *The Thinker* out of a rock. The sculptor chisels away a chunk of stone, shapes the curve of a kneecap, sands the forehead . . .

Now envision God doing the same: sculpting the way you are before you even were, engraving you with

> an eye for organization,
> an ear for fine music,
> a heart that beats for justice and fairness,
> a mind that understands quantum physics,
> the tender fingers of a caregiver,
> or the strong legs of a runner.

You cannot be anything you want to be. But you can be everything God wants you to be.

He made you *you-nique*.

Secular thinking, as a whole, doesn't buy this. Secular society sees no author behind the book, no architect behind the house, no purpose behind or beyond life. Society sees no bag and certainly never urges you to unpack one. It simply says, "You can be anything you want to be."

Be a butcher if you want to, a sales rep if you like. Be an ambassador if you really care. You can be anything you want to be. If you work hard enough. But can you? If God didn't pack within you the meat sense of a butcher, the people skills of a salesperson, or the world vision of an ambassador, can you be one? An unhappy, dissatisfied one perhaps. But a fulfilled one? No. Can an acorn become a rose, a whale fly like a bird, or lead become gold? Absolutely not. You cannot be anything you want to be. But you can be everything God wants you to be.

Søren Kierkegaard echoed the teaching of Scripture when he wrote, "At each man's birth there comes into being an eternal vocation for him, expressly for him. To be true to himself in relation to this eternal vocation is the highest thing a man can practice."[10]

PUT A SMILE ON
God's Face

*Don't live carelessly,
unthinkingly.
Make sure you understand
what the Master wants.*

EPHESIANS 5:17 MSG

GOD NEVER PREFABS or mass-produces people. No slapdash shaping. "I make all things new," he declares (Rev. 21:5). He didn't hand you your granddad's bag or your aunt's life; he personally and deliberately packed you. When you live out of the bag God gave, you discover an uncommon joy. Haven't you seen examples of this?

I recently flew to St. Louis on a commercial airline. The attendant was so grumpy I thought she'd had lemons for breakfast. She made her instructions clear: sit down, buckle up, and shut up! I dared not request anything lest she push the eject button.

Perhaps I caught her on the wrong day, or maybe she caught herself in the wrong career.

Two weeks later I took another flight. This attendant had been imported from heaven. She introduced herself to each passenger, had us greet each other, and then sang a song over the intercom! I had to ask her, "Do you like your work?"

"I love it!" she beamed. "For years I taught elementary school and relished each day. But then they promoted me. I went from a class of kids to an office of papers. Miserable! I resigned, took some months to study myself, found this opportunity, and snagged it. Now I can't wait to come to work!"

Too few people can say what she said. Few people do what she did. One job-placement firm suggests only 1 percent of its clients have made a serious study of their skills.[11]

Don't imitate their mistake. You can do something no one else can do in a fashion no one else can do it. Exploring and extracting your uniqueness excites you, honors God, and expands his kingdom. So "make a careful exploration of who you are and the work you have been given, and then sink yourself into that" (Gal. 6:4 MSG).

Discover and deploy your knacks.

Charlie Steinmetz did. He designed the generators that powered Henry Ford's first assembly lines in Dearborn, Michigan. Sometime after he retired, the generators stalled out, bringing the entire plant to a halt. Ford's engineers couldn't find the problem, so he called his old friend Charlie. Steinmetz fiddled with this gauge, jiggled that lever, tried this button, played with a few wires, and after a few hours threw the master switch. The motors kicked on, and the system returned to normal. Some days later Ford received a bill from Steinmetz for $10,000. Ford found the charge excessive and wrote his friend a note: "Charlie: It seems awfully steep, this $10,000, for a man who for just a little while tinkered around with a few motors." Steinmetz wrote a new bill and sent it back to Mr. Ford. "Henry: For tinkering around with motors, $10; for knowing where to tinker, $9,990."[12]

You tinker unlike anyone else. Explore and extract your tinker talent. A gift far greater than $10,000 awaits you. "Remember that the Lord will give a reward to everyone . . . for doing good" (Eph. 6:8 NCV).

When you do the most what you do the best, you put a smile on God's face. What could be better than that?

You can do something no one else can do in a fashion no one else can do it.

READ YOUR LIFE *Backward*

God is working in you to help you want to do and be able to do what pleases him.

EVERY SO often we find ourselves riding the flow of life. Not resisting or thrashing it, but just riding it. A stronger current lifts, channels, and carries, daring us to declare, "I was made to do this."

Do you know the flow? Sure you do.

Go back into your youth. What activity lured you off the gray sidewalk of sameness into an amusement park of sights, sounds, and colors? Oh, the fireworks. Every nerve ending buzzed; every brain cell sizzled; all five senses kicked in.

What were you doing? Assembling a model airplane in the garage? Helping your aunt plant seeds in the garden? Organizing games for your playground buddies? To this day you can remember the details of those days: the smell of cement glue, the feel of moist dirt, the squeals of excited kids. Magical. The only bad moment was the final moment.

Fast-forward a few years. Let childhood become adolescence, elementary school become middle school, then high school. Reflect on favorite memories: those full-flight moments of unclocked time and unlocked energy. All cylinders clicking. Again, what were you doing? What entranced you? Energized you? Engaged you?

If age and patience allow, indulge in one more pondering. Analyze your best days as a young adult. No upstream flailing. No battling against the current. During the times you rode the tide, what activities carried you? What objects did you hold? What topics did you consider?

Do you note common themes? To be sure, the scenery changes, and characters drop out. The details may alter, but your bent, your passion, what you yearn to do, you keep doing. The current of life's river keeps dropping you at a particular bank.

What is it that declares "I was made to do this"?

> Always fixing things,
> challenging systems,
> organizing facts,
> championing the small,
> networking behind the scenes,
> or seeking center stage.

Always doing the same thing.

And why not? It comes easily to you. Not without struggle, but with less struggle than your peers. You wondered why others found hitting a baseball or diagramming a sentence so difficult.

Anyone can assemble a television from a do-it-yourself kit, right?

Wrong. But David could. At the age of twelve, he did. He began the project with his dad. And when the navy called his father out to sea, David stayed at it. He spent after-school hours tracing diagrams, installing tubes, and soldering wires. By the time his father returned, the family had a new television.

To this day, a quarter of a century later, David's eyes still dance when he describes the moment the first image appeared on the screen. No surprise that he earned a degree in civil engineering. David loves to put stuff together.

He still does. Just ask the one hundred or so kids who attend Carver Academy, a state-of-the-art inner-city school in San Antonio. David Robinson built it. Yes, he played MVP-level basketball, but he also builds things. If the past is a teacher, he always will.

"The child is father of the man," wrote William Wordsworth. Want direction for the future? Then read your life backward.

OUR PAST
presents

OUR FUTURE

SOMETHING
You Enjoy

*In all your ways know, recognize,
and acknowledge Him,
and He will direct and make
straight and plain your paths.*

PROVERBS 3:6 AMP

JOB-PLACEMENT CONSULTANTS at People Management International Inc. have asked over seventy thousand clients this question: What things have you done in life that you enjoyed doing and believe you did well? "In every case," writes founder Arthur Miller Jr., "the data showed that people had invariably reverted to the same pattern of functioning whenever they had done something they enjoyed doing and did well."[13]

Or, to put it succinctly, our past presents our future. Can this be true? Can childhood interests forecast adult abilities? Can early leanings serve as first sketches of the final portrait?

Biographies of spiritual heroes suggest so. Start with the Egyptian prince. As a young man he excelled in the ways of the court. He mastered the laws of the ancient land. He studied at the feet of the world's finest astronomers, mathematicians, and lawyers. Fifteen hundred years later he was remembered as "learned in all the wisdom of the Egyptians, and . . . mighty in words and deeds" (Acts 7:22).

What little we know of Moses's upbringing tells us this: He displayed an affinity for higher learning and an allergy to injustice. Remember his first adult appearance in Scripture? He saw an Egyptian beating a Hebrew slave and killed the Egyptian. The next day Moses saw two Hebrews fighting and intervened again.

This time one of the Hebrews asked,

"Who made you a prince and a judge over us?"

A prince and a judge. How accurate is the description? Turn to the second act. To avoid arrest, Moses scampered into the badlands, where he encountered more injustice. "Now the priest of Midian had seven daughters. And they came and drew water, and they filled the troughs to water their father's flock. Then the shepherds came and drove them away; but Moses stood up and helped them, and watered their flock" (Exod. 2:16–17).

What drove Moses to protect these young women? Their beauty? His thirst? Maybe both or maybe more. Maybe irrepressible seeds of fairness grew in his soul. When he decked a cruel Egyptian or scattered chauvinistic shepherds, was he acting out his God-given bent toward justice?

The rest of his life would say so. Forty years after he fled Egypt, Moses returned, this time with God's burning-bush blessing and power. He dismantled Pharaoh and unshackled the Hebrews. Moses *the prince* escorted his people into a new kingdom. Moses *the judge* framed the Torah and midwifed the Hebrew law.

The strengths of his youth unveiled the passions of his life.

Our past presents our future.

STUDY YOUR
Mosaic

*Do not neglect
the gift that is in you . . .*

1 TIMOTHY 4:14

FAST-FORWARD past the life of Moses nearly two millenniums and consider another case. Like Moses, this young scholar displayed a youthful love of the law. He studied at the feet of Jerusalem's finest teachers. He followed the Torah with razor-sharp precision. He aligned himself with the Pharisees, ardent observers of Scripture. They defended the law with zeal. And "zeal" is the term he used to describe his youth. "Zealous?" he wrote. "Yes, in fact, I harshly persecuted the church" (Phil. 3:6 NLT).

Young Saul's ardor prompted his initial appearance in Scripture. Just like Moses, a murder brought him to the stage. Angry members of the Jewish council "cast [Stephen] out of the city and stoned him. And the witnesses laid down their clothes at the feet of a young man named Saul" (Acts 7:58).

Call Saul misguided, misled, or mistaken—but don't call Saul mild. If you scratched him, he bled commitment. Whether he was Saul, the legalist, or Paul, the apostle of grace, he couldn't sit still. Cause driven. Single-minded. Focused like a hawk on prey. Peter might tolerate the hypocrisy of the church. Not Paul. With him, you were either in or out, cold or hot. Whether persecuting disciples or making them, Paul impacted people.

An early strength forecast his lifelong trait.

Also consider the younger days of Billy Frank, the elder son of a dairy farmer. His dad rousted him out of bed around two thirty each morning to perform chores. Younger brother Melvin relished the work, tagging along at his father's side, eager to take his turn long before he was able.

Not Billy Frank. He and Melvin had the same father, but not the same bent. The minute he finished his chores, Billy Frank dashed into the hayloft with a copy of *Tarzan* or *Marco Polo*. By the age of fourteen, he had traced *The Decline and Fall of the Roman Empire*. Missionary stories, accounts of brave servants in faraway lands, fascinated the boy most of all.

An early strength forecasts a lifelong trait.

Later, as a college student at Florida Bible Institute, he visited with every evangelist who gave him time. He served their tables, polished their shoes, caddied for them, carried their luggage, posed to have his picture taken with them, and wrote home to tell his mother how much he "longed to be like this one or that one."[14]

Billy Frank bore one more trademark: energy. His mother remembered, "There was never any quietness about Billy. . . . I was relieved when he started school." He was hyperactive before the term existed. Always running, inquiring, questioning. "He never wears down," his parents told the doctor. "It's just the way he's built," the doctor assured.[15]

Study Billy Frank's mosaic: fascinated with books and words, intrigued by missionaries and faraway lands, blessed with boundless energy . . . What happens with a boy like that?

And what happens when God's Spirit convinces him of sin and salvation? Young Billy Frank decided to drop his middle name and go by his first. After all, an evangelist needs to be taken seriously. And people took Billy Frank Graham very seriously.

What if Graham had ignored his heart? What if his parents had forced him to stay on the farm? What if no one had noticed God's pattern in his life?

What if you fail to notice yours?

HEAVEN'S
Custom Design

*It is God himself who has made
us what we are and given us
new lives from Christ Jesus;
and long ages ago he planned
that we should spend these lives
in helping others.*

EPHESIANS 2:10 TLB

REMEMBER, God planned and packed you on purpose for his purpose. You are heaven's custom design. God "formed you in your mother's body" (Isa. 44:2 NCV). He determined your every detail. "Who made a person's mouth? And who makes someone deaf . . . ? Or who gives a person sight or blindness? It is I, the LORD" (Exod. 4:11 NCV).

At a moment before moments existed, the sovereign Star Maker resolved, "I will make _____." Your name goes in the blank. Then he continued with, "And I will make him/her _____ and _____ and _____ and _____." Fill those blanks with your characteristics. Insightful. Clever. Detail oriented. Restless. And since you are God's idea, you are a good idea. What God said about Jeremiah, he said about you: "Before I made you in your mother's womb, I chose you. Before you were born, I set you apart for a special work" (Jer. 1:5 NCV).

Set apart for a special work.

During a college break I made extra money by sweeping metal shavings.

Several dozen machinists spent ten hours a day shaping steel at their lathes. Need a six-inch square of quarter-inch sheet metal? They could cut it. Need screw holes in the hinge? They could bore them. Need a thin-stripped tin? Just tell the machinist. The workers shaped the steel according to its purpose. God does the same.

He shaped you according to yours.

God planned and packed you on purpose for his purpose.

How else can you explain yourself? Your ability to diagnose an engine problem by the noise it makes, to bake a cake without a recipe. You knew the Civil War better than your American history teacher. You know the name of every child in the orphanage. How do you explain such quirks of skill?

God. He knew young Israel would need a code, so he gave Moses a love for the law. He knew the doctrine of grace would need a fiery advocate, so he set Paul ablaze. And in your case, he knew what your generation would need and gave it. He designed you. And *his design defines your destiny*. Remember Peter's admonition? "If anyone ministers, let him do it as with the ability which God supplies" (1 Pet. 4:11).

I encountered walking proof of this truth on a trip to Central America. Dave,[16] a fellow American, was celebrating his sixty-first birthday with friends at the language school where my daughter was studying Spanish. My question— "What brings you here?"—opened a biographical floodgate. Drugs, sex, divorce, jail—Dave's first four decades read like a gangster's diary. But then God called him. Just as God called Moses, Paul, and millions, God called Dave.

His explanation went something like this. "I've always been able to fix things. All my life when stuff broke, people called me. A friend told me about poor children in Central America, so I came up with an idea. I find homes with no fathers and no plumbing. I install sinks and toilets and love kids. That's what I do. That's what I was made to do."

Sounds like Dave has found the cure for the common life. He's living in his sweet spot. What about you?

YOUR HEART'S
Desires

Delight yourself in the LORD
and he will give you
the desires of your heart.

PSALM 37:4 NIV

WHAT HAVE YOU always done well? And what have you always loved to do?

That last question trips up a lot of well-meaning folks. *God wouldn't let me do what I like to do—would he?* According to Paul, he would. "God is working in you to help you *want to do* and *be able to do* what pleases him" (Phil. 2:13 NCV). Your Designer couples the "want to" with the "be able to." Desire shares the driver's seat with ability. Your Father is too gracious to assign you to a life of misery. As Thomas Aquinas wrote, "Human life would seem to consist in that in which each man most delights, that for which he especially strives, and that which he particularly wishes to share with his friends."[17]

I recently met a twenty-year-old who needed to hear this. Just discharged from the military, he was pondering his future. He bore a square jaw, a forearm tattoo, and a common question. He didn't know what to do with the rest of his life. As we shared a flight, he told me about his uncle, a New England priest. "What a great man," the ex-soldier sighed. "He helps kids and feeds the hungry. I'd love to make a difference like that."

So I asked him the question of this chapter. "What were some occasions when you did something you love to do and did it well?"

He dismissed me at first.

"Aw, what I love to do is stupid."

"Try me," I invited.

"Well, I love to rebuild stuff."

"What do you mean?"

He spoke of an old coffee table he had found in a garage. Seeing its potential, he shaved off the paint, fixed the broken legs, and restored it. With great pride, he presented it to his mom.

"Tell me another time," I prompted.

The oak indwells the acorn.

"This one is really dumb," he discounted. "But when I worked at a butcher shop, I used to find meat on the bones others threw out. My boss loved me! I could find several pounds of product just by giving the bone a second try."

As the plane was nosing down, I tested a possibility with him. "You love to salvage stuff. You salvage furniture, salvage meat. God gave you the ability to find a treasure in someone else's trash."

My idea surprised him. "God? God did that?"

"Yes, God. Your ability to restore a table is every bit as holy as your uncle's ability to restore a life." You would have thought he'd just been handed a newborn baby. As my words sank in, the tough soldier teared up.

See your desires as gifts to heed rather than longings to suppress, and you'll feel the same joy.

So go ahead; reflect on your life. What have you always done well and loved to do?

Some find such a question too simple. Don't we need to measure something?[18] Aptitude or temperament? We consult teachers and tea leaves, read manuals and horoscopes. We inventory spiritual gifts[19] and ancestors. While some of these strategies might aid us, a simpler answer lies before us. Or, better stated, lies within us.

The oak indwells the acorn. Read your life backward and check your supplies. Rerelish your moments of success and satisfaction. For in the merger of the two, you find your uniqueness.

STUDY YOUR
S.T.O.R.Y.

The LORD looks from heaven;
He sees all the sons of men. . . .
He fashions their hearts individually;
He considers all their works.

PSALM 33:13, 15

CONSIDER THIS IDEA for a reality television show. The goal is simple. Each contestant must journey to a certain city, find a prescribed neighborhood, and assume a particular role. Call it *Find Your Place.*[20]

The fly in the ointment? No one tells you where to go or what to do when you get there. The host identifies no city. He designates no countries. He distributes no job descriptions. All contestants must discern their destinations by virtue of one tool. Their supplies. Upon leaving the starting spot, each one is handed a bag of supplies that provide the clues to that person's destination.

The host, for example, hands one person a cowhide bag crammed with sweaters, a parka, and a soccer ball. In the side pocket, the contestant finds coins. Argentine currency. A teacher's attendance sheet from a language school. Looks like the destination and position are shaping up.

Another is given diving equipment. Oxygen tanks. Fins and goggles. Someone is going near an ocean. And what's this? A wrench? Deep-sea divers don't carry tools. Wait, here is yet another clue. A book. Diagrams of offshore drilling rigs. This person seems to be headed to a drilling platform.

Networks won't syndicate the show, you say? Too boring?

Take your concern to the originator of the plot. God.

He developed the story line and enlisted you as a participant.

You didn't exit the womb with your intended career tattooed on your chest. No printout of innate skills accompanied your birth. But as life progressed, you began noticing your gifts. Skills, revealed. Knacks, uncovered.

God gave those. "It is God himself who has made us what we are and given us new lives from Christ Jesus; and long ages ago he planned that we should spend these lives in helping others" (Eph. 2:10 TLB).

The cure for commonness begins with strength extraction. No one else has your skill makeup. Disregard it at your peril. An oil-rig repairman won't feel at home in an Argentine schoolroom. And if God made you to teach Argentine kids, you won't enjoy offshore derrick repair. And the kids in the class and the workers on the platform? Don't they want the right person in the right place? Indeed, they do. You do too. And, most of all, God does. You are the only you he made.

In their book *Behavioral Genetics*, a team of scientists declare:

> Each of us has the capacity to generate 10^{3000} eggs or sperm with unique sets of genes. If we consider 10^{3000} possible eggs being generated by an individual woman and the same number of sperm being generated by an individual man, the likelihood of anyone else with your set of genes in the past or in the future becomes infinitesimal.[21]

If numbers numb you, let me simplify. God made you and broke the mold. "The LORD looks from heaven; He sees all the sons of men. From the place of His dwelling He looks on all the inhabitants of the earth; *He fashions their hearts individually;* He considers all their works" (Ps. 33:13–15). Every single baby is a brand-new idea from the mind of God.

Scan history for your replica; you won't find it. God tailor-made you. He "personally formed and made each one" (Isa. 43:7 MSG). No box of "backup yous" sits in God's workshop. You aren't one of many bricks in the mason's pile or one of a dozen bolts in the mechanic's drawer. You are it! And if you aren't you, we don't get you. The world misses out.

You are heaven's Halley's comet; we have one shot at seeing you shine. You offer a gift to society that no one else brings. If you don't bring it, it won't be brought.

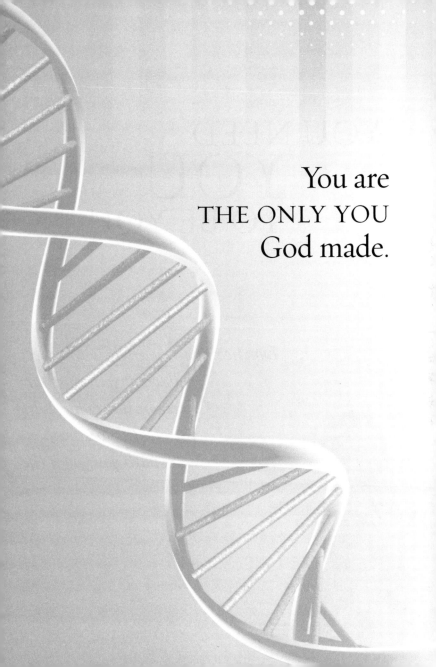

You are
THE ONLY YOU
God made.

YOU NEED
YOU
TO BE YOU

*Don't compare yourself with others.
Each of you must take
responsibility for doing
the creative best you can
with your own life.*

GALATIANS 6:4–5 MSG

I JOGGED through my neighborhood the other day under a cloud. Not a cloud of rain, but a cloud of self-doubt. The challenges of life seemed to outnumber the resources, and I questioned my ability. And, quite frankly, I questioned God's wisdom. *Are you sure I'm the right man for this job?* was the theme of my prayer.

Apparently God really wanted to give me an answer, because I heard one. From on high. From a deep, booming voice. "You're doing a good job!" I stopped dead in my Reeboks and looked up. Seeing nothing in the clouds, I shifted my attention to the roof of a house. There he waved at me—a painter dressed in white and leaning against a dormer. I waved back. And I wondered and almost asked, "How did you know I needed to hear that?"

Did I have a brush with an angel? Did I see an angel with a brush? Was the worker sunstruck? This much I know. A painter spots a middle-aged guy with a bald spot puffing through the streets and thinks, *The guy could use a good word.* So he gives it. "You're doing a good job!"

Am I stretching theology

a bit when I suggest that God put the man there, at least in part, for me?

Long before time had time, God saw each moment in time, including that one. He saw a minister in need of a word. He saw a fellow with a skill for painting and a heart for encouragement. He put one on the street and the other on the roof so the second could encourage the first. Multiply that tiny event by billions, and behold the way God sustains his world. "God, who makes everything work together, will work you into his most excellent harmonies" (Phil. 4:9 MSG).

The Unseen Conductor prompts this orchestra we call living. When gifted teachers aid struggling students and skilled managers

You play no small part, because there is no small part to be played.

disentangle bureaucratic knots, when dog lovers love dogs and number-crunchers zero balance the account, when you and I do the most what we do the best for the glory of God, we are "marvelously functioning parts in Christ's body" (Rom. 12:5 MSG).

You play no small part, because there is no small part to be played. "All of you together are Christ's body, and each one of you is a separate and necessary part of it" (1 Cor. 12:27 NLT). "Separate" and "necessary." Unique and essential. No one else has been given your lines. God "shaped each person in turn" (Ps. 33:15 MSG). The Author of the human drama entrusted your part to you alone. Live your life, or it won't be lived. We need you to be you.

You need you to be you.

You can't be your hero, your parent, or your big brother. You might imitate their golf swing or hairstyle, but you can't be them. You can only be you. All you have to give is what you've been given to give. Concentrate on who you are and what you have.

Be the Best
YOU CAN BE

*I would remind you to stir up
(rekindle the embers of,
fan the flame of, and keep burning)
the [gracious] gift of God,
[the inner fire] that is in . . .*

2 TIMOTHY 1:6 AMP

BEFORE THOMAS MERTON followed Christ, he followed money, fame, and society. He shocked many when he exchanged it all for the life of a Trappist monk in a Kentucky monastery. Business-world colleagues speculated what he must have become. They envisioned a silenced, suffering version of their friend dutifully sludging through a life of penance. After thirteen years, a colleague, Mark van Doren, visited him and then reported back to the others: "He looked a little older; but as we sat and talked I could see no important difference in him, and once I interrupted a reminiscence of his by laughing. 'Tom,' I said, 'you haven't changed at all.' 'Why should I? Here,' he said, 'our duty is to be more ourselves, not less.'"[22]

God never called you to be anyone other than you. But he does call on you to be the best *you* you can be. The big question is, at your best, who are you?

A group of kids were sitting together at the movie theater when one decided to go to the concession stand. Upon re-entering the theater, he couldn't find his group. He walked up and down the aisles, growing more confused with each step. Finally he stood in front of the theater and shouted, "Does anybody recognize me?"

Have you asked kindred questions? Does anyone know who I am? Where I belong? Where I'm supposed to go?

If so, it's time to study your S.T.O.R.Y. and find out.

Strengths

Topics

Optimal Conditions

Relationships

Yes!

WHAT ARE YOUR
Strengths?

*God has given each
of us the ability to do
certain things well.*

ROMANS 12:6 NLT

GOD GAVE YOU, not a knapsack, but a knack sack. These knacks accomplish results. Maybe you have a knack for managing multitudes of restaurant orders or envisioning solutions to personnel issues. Synonymous verbs mark your biography: "repairing," "creating," "overseeing." Perhaps you decipher things—Sanskrit or football defenses. Maybe you organize things—data or butterflies. I found my youngest daughter reorganizing her closet, again. *Is this my child?* I wondered. She straightens her closet more often in one month than her father has straightened his in his life! Will she someday do the same in a classroom, medical clinic, or library?

Strengths—you employ them often with seemingly little effort. An interior decorator told me this about her work: "It's not that hard. I walk into a room and begin to see what it needs."

"Not all of us see it," I told her. I can't even decorate my bed. But she can redecorate a garbage dump. Bingo! Knowing her strength led her to her sweet spot. And people pay her to live there!

What certain things come to you so easily that you genuinely wonder why others can't do them? Doesn't everyone know the periodic table of elements? Nooooo, they don't. But the fact that you do says much about your strength (not to mention your IQ!). It also says something about your topic.

Knowing your strength leads to your sweet spot.

WHAT IS
Your Topic?

*Moses summoned Bezalel
and Oholiab and every skilled person
to whom the LORD had given
ability and who was willing
to come and do the work.*

EXODUS 36:2

ONCE YOU KNOW YOUR VERBS, look for your nouns. What objects do you enjoy working with? Animals? Statistics? People? Your topic can be as abstract as an idea or as concrete as fruit. Arthur Miller Jr. has a friend fascinated by fruit. "Henry," he writes, "not only knows his products, he's downright passionate about them." Miller continues:

> He starts his day in the middle of the night at the wholesale market, buying only high-priced, very good quality produce. He will not buy the ordinary. It is why people come from long distances, and sometimes in chauffeured cars, to tap Henry's passion. His wife says he is a "maniac" about his work. I'll visit Henry to buy a couple of melons, and lightly squeezing a couple of dandies ask, "Are these ripe?" "Not yet!" Henry declares. "Gotta wait until tomorrow." Then he adds, mischievously, "About three o'clock!"
>
> I think he's only half kidding. I think . . . he really does know almost the exact instant when a piece of fruit becomes perfectly ripe! . . .
>
> Imagine if everyone could find the same intensity as . . . Henry Balsamo.[23]

God implants such passion.

Listen to the way he described the builder Bezalel. "I have filled him with the Spirit of God, giving him great wisdom, intelligence, and skill in all kinds of crafts. He is able to create beautiful objects from gold, silver, and bronze. He is skilled in cutting and setting gemstones and in carving wood. Yes, he is a master at every craft!" (Exod. 31:3–5 NLT).

That's God speaking! Can you hear the pleasure in his voice? He sounds like a grandpa flipping photos out of his wallet. "I have filled him . . . He is able . . . He is skilled . . . Yes, he is a master." When you do the most what you do the best, you pop the pride buttons on the vest of God.

WHAT FASCINATION
did he give you?

*What makes
your pulse race
and your eyebrow arch?*

GOD IMPLANTS *passion*

WHAT ARE *Your Optimal Conditions?*

*Each one should use
whatever gift he has received
to serve others,
faithfully administering God's grace
in its various forms.*

1 PETER 4:10 NIV

WHAT FACTORS trigger your motivation? Some people love to respond to a need. Others are motivated by problems. A competent bookkeeper likely thrives under predictable routine. The firefighter relishes a day packed with different surprises.

So does Dennis McDonald. For a time he served as the business director of our church. He did a fine job. As an elder, however, he often visited the sick. I noticed a distinct difference in enthusiasm when Dennis described his hospital work and his office work. In the office, Dennis soldiered on. He did a fine job managing the routine, but send him to the bedside of the sick, and hear his tone elevate. His optimal setting is crisis, so it made sense to move him from administrator to full-time hospital pastor. A 9-1-1 situation starts his engine.

What starts yours?

Building or maintaining?
Clearly defined structure or open-ended possibilities?
Assembly-line assignments?
Boundaryless opportunities?

What are your optimal conditions?

What starts your engine?

WHAT ABOUT
Relationships?

*Each man has his own
gift from God;
one has this gift,
another has that.*

1 CORINTHIANS 7:7 NIV

THINK BACK over your moments of satisfaction and success. On those days, how were you relating to people?

Some seek out a team, a club, a society. When it comes to yard work, they want the whole family to be outside. Some people are stimulated by groups.

Others function better alone. They pass on the community softball teams or bowling leagues. They prefer to hike or fly-fish or play golf. It's not that they don't like people but more that they don't need people to achieve their assignment.

Still others enjoy a group, but they have to lead the group. In fact, they can't not lead the group. They may come across as pushy or domineering, but they don't mean to. They just see what others will see but don't see yet.

Know your ideal relationship pattern. If you like to energize others but your job plops you in front of a computer screen, your days will pass with ice-floe speed. Diagnose your relationship style, and, one final element, determine your payday.

Know your ideal relationship pattern.

YES!

*But by the grace of God
I am what I am,
and His grace toward me
was not in vain.*

1 CORINTHIANS 15:10

IN THE MOVIE *Chariots of Fire*, Eric Liddell defended his devotion to running by telling his sister, "God made me fast, and when I run, I feel his pleasure." When do you feel God's pleasure? When do you look up into the heavens and say, "I was made to do this"? When do your Strengths, Topic, Optimal conditions, and Relationship pattern converge in such a fashion that you say, "Yes!"? When they do, you are living out your S.T.O.R.Y.

Incarnate yours. Accept God's permission to be whom he made you to be. A frog can flap its little legs and never fly. Some of you have been flapping a long time—too long. Your heroes are birds; your mentors are birds. You think you should fly and feel guilty that you can't. Enough of this bird-brained thinking. Be a frog! It's okay to jump. You have some studdish thighs beneath you, so get hopping.

Do you know who you are?

The time you spend quarrying your God-granted skills is well used.

Rick Burgess and Bill "Bubba" Bussey host the wildly popular Rick and Bubba Show, a drive-time radio broadcast that originates in Birmingham, Alabama.

Animators once made a cartoon out of the two characters and invited Rick and Bubba to provide the voices. Rick was the voice of Rick, and Bubba, the voice of Bubba. Bubba, however, couldn't seem to please his producer. He suggested that Bubba change inflections, volume, and other details. Bubba grew understandably impatient. After all, he was voicing himself. He turned to the producer and objected, "If I am me, how can I mess me up?"[24]

Great point. When it comes to being you, you were made for the part. So speak your lines with confidence.

Incarnate your S.T.O.R.Y.

DON'T CONSULT
Your Greed

*Be content with who you are,
and don't put on airs.
God's strong hand is on you;
he'll promote you at the right time.*

1 PETER 5:6 MSG

A BUSINESSMAN bought popcorn from an old street vendor each day after lunch. He once arrived to find the peddler closing up his stand at noon. "Is something wrong?" he asked.

A smile wrinkled the seller's leathery face. "By no means. All is well."

"Then why are you closing your popcorn stand?"

"So I can go to my house, sit on my porch, and sip tea with my wife."

The man of commerce objected. "But the day is still young. You can still sell."

"No need to," the stand owner replied. "I've made enough money for today."

"Enough? Absurd. You should keep working."

The spry old man stopped and stared at his well-dressed visitor. "And why should I keep working?"

"To sell more popcorn."

"And why sell more popcorn?"

"Because the more popcorn you sell, the more money you make. The more money you make, the richer you are. The richer you are, the more popcorn stands you can buy. The more popcorn stands you buy, the more peddlers sell your product, and the richer you become. And when you have enough, you can stop working, sell your popcorn stands, stay home, and sit on the porch with your wife and drink tea."

The popcorn man smiled. "I can do that today. I guess I have enough."

When is enough enough?

DON'T RISK
Losing Your
Purpose

Be on your guard against every form of greed.

LUKE 12:15 NASB

| 98 |

I'M RICH ENOUGH—A phrase on the verge of extinction. We love to supersize our french fries, television screens, and closets—and I've wondered what my dad would say about my penchant for $3.45 lattes.

Who could disagree with Linda Kulman, who wrote:

We are a nation that believes in having it all. In 1950, American families owned one car and saved for a second. In 2000, nearly 1 in 5 families owned three cars or more. . . . Americans shell out more for garbage bags than 90 of the world's 210 countries spend for everything. Indeed, America has double the number of shopping malls as it does high schools.[25]

In 1900 the average person living in the United States wanted seventy-two different things and considered eighteen of them essential. Today the average person wants five hundred things and considers one hundred of them essential.[26]

Our obsession with stuff carries a hefty price tag. The average American family devotes a full one-fourth of its spendable income to outstanding debts.[27] We spend 110 percent of our disposable income trying to manage debt.[28] And who can keep up?

We no longer measure ourselves against the Joneses next door

Greed has a growling stomach.

but against the star on the screen or the stud on the magazine cover. Hollywood's diamonds make yours look like a gumball-machine toy. Who can satisfy Madison Avenue? No one can.

Greed comes in many forms. Greed for approval. Greed for applause. Greed for status. Greed for the best office, the fastest car, the prettiest date. Greed has many faces, but speaks one language: the language of more. Epicurus noted, "Nothing is enough for the man to whom enough is too little." And what was that observation of John D. Rockefeller's? He was asked, "How much money does it take to satisfy a man?" He answered, "Just a little more."[29] Wise was the one who wrote, "Whoever loves money never has money enough; whoever loves wealth is never satisfied with his income" (Eccles. 5:10 NIV).

Greed has a growling stomach. Feed it, and you risk more than budget-busting debt. You risk losing purpose. Greed can seduce the best.

You've seen it happen. The popcorn peddler in the previous reading has one stand and one job and manages both with skill. But though his daily sales meet his needs, they don't meet his tastes. To make more money, he buys more stands; to supervise the stands, he abandons his own.

The street vendor no longer sells; he manages. Which is fine, if he was made to manage. But suppose he was made to sell. Suppose he swaps the open street and river of people for four walls and a desk. Will he give up more than he gains?

IS THE PROMOTION
a Promotion?

*I have learned the secret of being
content in any and every situation,
whether well fed or hungry,
whether living in plenty or in want.*

PHILIPPIANS 4:12

GOD'S ANSWER lies in Scripture's first parable. Long before readers pondered the stories of the prodigal son and the good Samaritan, they reflected on the parable of the trees.

Jotham tells the story. He is a son of Gideon and the sole survivor of a seventy-man massacre. Abimelech authorized the slaughter. He sought to kill any person who might keep him from the throne. Jotham comes out of hiding just long enough to address the citizens of Israel and tell them this story:

> Once upon a time the trees decided to elect a king. First they said to the olive tree, "Be our king!" But it refused, saying, "Should I quit producing the olive oil that blesses both God and people, just to wave back and forth over the trees?"
>
> Then they said to the fig tree, "You be our king!" But the fig tree also refused, saying, "Should I quit producing my sweet fruit just to wave back and forth over the trees?"
>
> Then they said to the grapevine, "You be our king!" But the grapevine replied, "Should I quit producing the wine that cheers both God and people, just to wave back and forth over the trees?"

Then all the trees finally turned

In a desire to be great, one might cease being any good.

to the thornbush and said, "Come, you be our king!" And the thornbush replied, "If you truly want to make me your king, come and take shelter in my shade. If not, let fire come out from me and devour the cedars of Lebanon." (Judg. 9:8–15 NLT)

Via the parable, Jotham warns the Israelites against thorny Abimelech. Via the parable, God warns us against greed-driven promotions.

The trees entice the olive tree, fig tree, and grapevine with a throne-room invitation: "Reign over us!" One by one they refuse the offer. The olive tree wants to keep giving oil. The fig tree wants to keep giving figs, and the vine wants to keep bearing grapes. All refuse to pay the price of promotion.

These plants take pride in their posts. Why abandon fruitfulness? In the end, only the thornbush takes the offer. Be careful, the story instructs. *In a desire to be great, one might cease being any good.*

Not every teacher is equipped to be a principal.

Not every carpenter has the skill to head a crew.

Not every musician should conduct an orchestra.

Promotions might promote a person right out of his or her sweet spot. For the love of more, we might lose our purpose.

If trees offer you royalty, you don't have to take it.

IN A DESIRE

TO BE GREAT,

one might cease being any good

STICK WITH YOUR
S.T.O.R.Y.

*You, LORD, give perfect peace
to those who keep their purpose firm
and put their trust in you.*

ISAIAH 26:3 TEV

JUST BECAUSE a king gives you armor, you don't have to wear it. David didn't. When he volunteered to go mano a mano with Goliath, King Saul tried to clothe the shepherd boy with soldier's armor. After all, Goliath stood over nine feet tall. He wore a bronze helmet and a 125-pound coat of mail. He bore bronze leggings and carried a javelin and a spear with a 15-pound head (1 Sam. 17:4–7 NLT). And David? David had a slingshot. This is a VW Bug playing blink with an eighteen-wheeler, a salmon daring the grizzly to bring it on. When Saul saw David, pimpled, and Goliath, rippled, he did what any Iron Age king would do. "Saul gave David his own armor—a bronze helmet and a coat of mail" (1 Sam. 17:38 NLT).

But David refused it. Look at this wise young man. "David put it on, strapped the sword over it, and took a step or two to see what it was like, for he had never worn such things before. 'I can't go in these,' he protested. 'I'm not used to them.' So he took them off again" (v. 39 NLT).

David rejected the armor,

selected the stones, lobotomized the giant, and taught us a powerful lesson: What fits others might not fit you. Indeed, what fits t*he king* might not fit you. Just because someone hands you armor, you don't have to wear it. Just because someone gives you advice, a job, or a promotion, you don't have to accept it. Let your uniqueness define your path of life.

Examine your gifts; know your strengths. "Have a sane estimate of your capabilities" (Rom. 12:3 PHILLIPS). When someone tries to bump you out of your sweet spot, here is your rebuttal: "This is my S.T.O.R.Y., and I'm sticking to it."

Don't heed greed.

Greed makes a poor job counselor. She tells fig trees to bear no figs, olive trees to bear no oil, vines to bear no grapes. Don't consult her. "Don't be obsessed with getting more material things. Be relaxed with what you have" (Heb. 13:5 MSG). Is not the right job with little better than the wrong job with much? "It is better to have little with fear for the LORD than to have great treasure with turmoil" (Prov. 15:16 NLT). As the Japanese proverb says, "Even if you sleep in a thousand-mat room, you can only sleep on one mat."[30]

Greed makes a poor job counselor.

CONSULT YOUR
Designer

*Godliness with contentment
is great gain.*

1 TIMOTHY 6:6 NIV

DON'T LET THE ITCH for things or the ear for applause derail you from your God-intended design.

In his book *Money: A User's Manual*, Bob Russell describes a farmer who once grew discontent with his farm. He griped about the lake on his property always needing to be stocked and managed. The hills humped his roads, forcing him to drive up and down. And those fat cows lumbered through his pasture. All the fencing and feeding—what a headache!

He decided to sell the place and move somewhere nice. He called a real-estate agent and made plans to list the farm. A few days later the agent phoned, wanting approval for the advertisement she intended to place in the local paper. She read the ad to the farmer. It described a lovely farm in an ideal location—quiet and peaceful, contoured with rolling hills, carpeted with soft meadows, nourished by a fresh lake, and blessed with well-bred livestock. The farmer said, "Read that ad to me again."

After hearing it a second time, he said, "I've changed my mind. I'm not going to sell. I've been looking for a place like that all my life."[31]

Paul would have applauded that farmer.

He learned the same lesson: "I have learned in whatever state I am, to be content" (Phil. 4:11).

Before you change your job title, examine your perspective toward life.

Success is not defined by position or pay scale but by this: doing the most what you do the best.

Parents, give that counsel to your kids. Tell them to do what they love to do so well that someone pays them to do it.

Spouses, urge your mate to choose satisfaction over salary. Better to be married to a happy person who has a thin wallet than a miserable person with a thick one. Besides, "a pretentious, showy life is an empty life; a plain and simple life is a full life" (Prov. 13:7 MSG).

Pursue the virtue of contentment. When choosing or changing jobs, be careful. Consult your design. Consult your Designer. But never consult your greed.

Success is not defined by position
or pay scale but by this:
doing the most what you do the best.

TAKE GREAT RISKS
for God

*And to one he gave five talents,
to another two, and to another
one, to each according to his
own ability; and immediately
he went on a journey.*

MATTHEW 25:15

BEFORE "TALENT" meant skill, it meant money. It represented the largest unit of accounting in the Greek currency—10,000 denarii.[32] According to the parable of the workers, a denarius represented a day's fair wages (Matt. 20:2). Multiply your daily wage by 10,000, and you discover the value of a talent. If you earn $30,000 a year and you annually work 260 days, you make about $115 a day. A talent in your case is valued at 10,000 times $115, or $1,150,000.

Place this in perspective. Suppose a person earns $30,000 a year for forty years. Her lifetime earnings are $1,200,000, only $50,000 more than a talent. One talent, then, equals a lifetime of earnings. This is a lot of money and a key point in this parable. Your God-given design and uniqueness have high market value in heaven. God didn't entrust you with a $2 talent or a $5 skill.

Consider yourself a million-dollar investment—in many cases, a multimillion-dollar enterprise.

God gives gifts, not miserly, but abundantly.

And not randomly, but carefully: "to each according to each one's unique ability" (v. 15).[33]

Remember, no one else has your talents. No one. God elevates you from commonhood by matching your unique abilities to custom-made assignments.

In the parable the first two

servants rewarded their master's trust. "Immediately the one who had received the five talents went and traded with them, and gained five more talents. In the same manner the one who had received the two talents gained two more" (vv. 16–17 NASB).

The five-talent servant jumped to the task. He "went and traded" the money. He bought investment magazines and watched the business channel. A reliable tip led him to examine some property. He heard about a franchise looking for capital. He pondered his options, crunched the numbers, took a gulp, and took the plunge. He invested the money.

The second servant showed equal eagerness. He may have had only two talents, but, by George, he put them to work. Like the first servant, he negotiated, traded, and invested.

The only mistake is not to risk making one.

Both took risks. Both dared to fail. Who was to say their investments wouldn't NASDAQ into pennies? No one. But they took the chance nonetheless.

And their master heaped praise upon them. When he returned from his journey, he applauded the five-talent man and two-talent man equally: "Well done, good and faithful servant" (v. 21, 23). He altered no phrase and omitted no honor. The two-talent servant who faithfully fills soda cups for the homeless receives the same applause as the five-talent evangelist who fills stadiums with people. Different fruit, equal praise.

The point? Use your uniqueness to take great risks for God!

If you're great with kids, volunteer at the orphanage.

If you have a head for business, start a soup kitchen.

If God bent you toward medicine, dedicate a day or a decade to AIDS patients.

TRUST
Little Deeds

*Do not despise these
small beginnings.*

ZECHARIAH 4:10 NLT

DO YOU SENSE that the divine spark within is beginning to flame? Should you douse it or fan it? Dare you dream that you can make a difference in this world?

God's answer would be, "Just do something and see what happens."

That's what he told the citizens of ancient Jerusalem. For sixteen years the temple of God had lain in ruins. They had abandoned the work. The reason? Opposition from enemies, indifference from neighbors. But most of all, the job dwarfed them. To build the first temple, Solomon had needed seventy thousand carriers, eighty thousand stonecutters, thirty-three hundred foremen, and seven years. A gargantuan task! The workers must have thought, *What difference will my work make?* God's answer: "Do not despise these small beginnings, for the LORD rejoices to see the work begin" (Zech. 4:10 NLT).

Begin. Just begin! What seems small to you might be huge to someone else. Just ask Bohn Fawkes. During World War II, he piloted a B-17. On one mission he sustained flak from Nazi antiaircraft guns. Even though his gas tanks were hit, the plane did not explode, and Fawkes was able to land the plane.

On the morning following the raid, Fawkes asked his crew chief for the German shell.

He wanted to keep a souvenir of his incredible good fortune. The crew chief explained that not just one but eleven shells had been found in the gas tanks, none of which had exploded.

Technicians opened the missiles and found them void of explosive charge. They were clean and harmless and with one exception, empty. The exception contained a carefully rolled piece of paper. On it a message had been scrawled in the Czech language. Translated, the note read: "This is all we can do for you now."[34]

A courageous assembly-line worker was disarming bombs and scribbled the note. He couldn't end the war, but he could save one plane. He couldn't do everything, but he could do something. So he did it.

God does big things with small deeds.

Just do something and see what happens.

CHANGE THE *World*

The Kingdom of Heaven is like
a mustard seed planted in a field.
It is the smallest of all seeds,
but it becomes the largest of garden plants;
it grows into a tree,
and birds come and make nests
in its branches.

MATTHEW 13:31–32 NLT

AGAINST A TOWERING GIANT, a brook pebble seems futile. But God used it to topple Goliath. Compared to the tithes of the wealthy, a widow's coins seem puny. But Jesus used them to inspire us. And in contrast with sophisticated priests and powerful Roman rulers, a cross-suspended carpenter seemed nothing but a waste of life. Few Jewish leaders mourned his death. Only a handful of friends buried his body. The people turned their attention back to the temple. Why not?

What power does a buried rabbi have? We know the answer. Mustard-seed and leaven-lump power. Power to tear away death rags and push away death rocks. Power to change history. In the hands of God, small seeds grow into sheltering trees. Tiny leaven expands into nourishing loaves.

Small deeds can change the world. Sow the mustard seed. Bury the leaven lump. Make the call. Write the check. Organize the committee.

Chief Wiggles noticed a little girl crying on the other side

of a stretch of barbed wire in Baghdad. "She was obviously very poor, in her tattered old dress, totally worn-out plastic flip-flops, her hair matted against her head indicating she hadn't had a bath in a long time and her skin blistered from the dirt and weather." The soldier remembered some toys in his office, so he hurried and brought the girl a toothbrush, whistle, and toy monkey. As he gave the gifts, "her eyes lit up with such joy." He posted this experience on his Weblog, and thousands of people responded, asking where they could send gifts. Operation Give was born. And the soldier inherited Halvorsen's nickname—"Chief Wiggles."[35]

Don't discount the smallness of your deeds.

Moses had a staff.

David had a sling.

Samson had a jawbone.

Rahab had a string.

Mary had some ointment.

Aaron had a rod.

Dorcas had a needle.

All were used by God.

What do you have?

God inhabits the tiny seed, empowers the tiny deed. He cures the common life by giving no common life, by offering no common gifts. "Do all the good you can, by all the means you can, in all the ways you can, in all the places you can, at all the times you can, to all the people you can, as long as ever you can."[36] Don't discount the smallness of your deeds.

ENDNOTES

[1] Frederick Dale Bruner, *Matthew: A Commentary*, vol. 2, *The Churchbook: Matthew 13–28* (Dallas: Word, 1990), 902.

[2] Martin Buber, *The Way of Man, According to the Teaching of Hasidism* (London: Routledge Classics, 1994), vi. Jewish theologian Martin Buber writes: "The world is an irradiation of God, but as it is endowed with an independence of existence and striving, it is apt, always and everywhere, to form a crust around itself. Thus, *a divine spark* lives in every thing and being, but each such spark is enclosed by an isolating shell. Only man can liberate it and re-join it with the Origin: by holding holy converse with the thing and using it in a holy manner, that is, so that his intention in doing so remains directed towards God's transcendence. Thus the divine immanence emerges from the exile of the 'shells'" (emphasis mine).

[3] "'Red, White & Blue' Students to Present Check to NYC Police, Firemen Nov. 9," Texas A&M University, http://www.tamu.edu/univrel/ aggiedaily/news/ stories/01/110201-10.

[4] U.S. Bureau of Labor Statistics, 1998.

[5] National Institute for Occupational Safety and Health, "Stress at Work," http://www.cdc. gov/niosh/stresswk.html.

[6] Arthur F. Miller Jr. with William Hendricks, *The Power of Uniqueness: How to Become Who You Really Are* (Grand Rapids: Zondervan, 1999), 21.

[7] Ellen Galinsky, Stacy S. Kim, and James T. Bond, *Feeling Overworked: When Work Becomes Too Much* (New York: Families and Work Institute, 2001), 11.

[8] Nicholas Lore, *The Pathfinder: How to Choose or Change Your Career for a Lifetime of Satisfaction and Success* (New York: Simon & Schuster, 1998), 11.

[9] National Institute for Occupational Safety and Health, "Stress at Work."

[10] Søren Kierkegaard, *Purity of Heart Is to Will One Thing: Spiritual Preparation for the Office of Confession*, 140, quoted in Miller with Hendricks, *The Power of Uniqueness*, 251.

[11] Miller with Hendricks, *The Power of Uniqueness*, 30.

[12] Charles R. Swindoll, *The Tale of the Tardy Oxcart and 1,501 Other Stories* (Nashville: Word, 1998), 321–22.

[13] Miller with Hendricks, *The Power of Uniqueness*, 46.

[14] William Martin, *A Prophet with Honor: The Billy Graham Story* (New York: William Morrow and Co., 1991), 71.

[15] Ibid., 57.

[16] Not his actual name.

[17] Saint Thomas Aquinas, *Summa Theologia*, quoted in Miller with Hendricks, *The Power of Uniqueness*, 250.

[18] Any measurement tool is limited in scope. It seeks to place the personality in a grid, box, or grouping. If each person functions in a unique fashion, a test would need a category for each human being. None can provide this.

[19] New Testament gift listings are, in my opinion, to be seen as samplings. If they are conclusive, no early church saw the entire list. Rome saw one part, Corinth another, and Peter's audience yet a third. A better option is to see the lists as examples of spiritual skills. Caution, then, is to be taken with spiritual gift inventories. They might *suggest* a gift mix, but can't define one.

[20] Here is the theme song: "Come join the RA-AACE To find your PLA-AACE. Your bag has CLU-UES, Packed just for YOU-OUS . . . guys." Okay—theme songs aren't my sweet spot.

[21] Robert Plomin, J. C. DeFries, and G. E. McClearn, *Behavioral Genetics: A Primer* (New York: W. H. Freeman, 1990), 314, quoted in James Hillman, *The Soul's Code: In Search of Character and Calling* (New York: Random House, 1996), 137.

[22] Monica Furlong, *Merton: A Biography* (San Francisco: HarperCollins, 1980), 225.

[23] Miller with Hendricks, *The Power of Uniqueness*, 55.

[24] My thanks to Rick Burgess and Bill "Bubba" Bussey of the *Rick and Bubba Show* from Birmingham, Alabama, for granting permission to use this story.

[25] Linda Kulman, "Our Consuming Interest," *U.S. News & World Report*, June 28–July 5, 2004, 59.

[26] Bob Russell with Rusty Russell, *Money: A User's Manual* (Sisters, OR: Multnomah, 1997), 82.

[27] Larry Burkett, *Using Your Money Wisely: Guidelines from Scripture* (Chicago: Moody Press, 1986), 76.

[28] Kulman, "Our Consuming Interest," 59.

[29] Russell with Russell, *Money*, 50–51.

[30] Paul Lee Tan, *Encyclopedia of 7,700 Illustrations: Signs of the Times* (Rockville, MD: Assurance Publishers, 1979), 273, #839.

[31] Russell with Russell, *Money*, 69.

[32] Bruner, *Matthew: A Commentary*, vol. 2, *The Churchbook: Matthew 13–28*, 902.

[33] Ibid.

[34] Elmer Bendiner, *The Fall of Fortresses: A Personal Account of the Most Daring—and Deadly—American Air Battles of World War II* (New York: G. P. Putnam's Sons, 1980), 138–39.

[35] "Chief Wiggles (2003, Operation Give)," Operation Give, www.operationgive.org.

[36] John Wesley, http://www.myquotations. net/?QuoteID-58602.